CITY of ETERNAL SPRING

Afaa Michael Weaver

蔚 雅 風

UNIVERSITY OF PITTSBURGH PRESS

Published by the University of Pittsburgh Press, Pittsburgh, Pa., 15260
Copyright © 2014, Afaa Michael Weaver
All rights reserved
Manufactured in the United States of America
Printed on acid-free paper
10 9 8 7 6 5 4 3 2 1
ISBN 13: 978-0-8229-6325-7
ISBN 10: 0-8229-6325-6

in
loving memory
Michael S. Weaver Jr.
1971–1972

心聲音

要聽到心聲音

幫我忘了以往

幫我忘了未來

Contents

III. Memories

IV. Intimacies

V. Soul Space

I. Map of the Heart

What the Lotus Said

It will hurt when the knife is pulled away,
pain no longer my walking staff and candle,
mist taking over where doctors and medication
once were the compromise with being born,
stuck down in the algae of a coral reef, mind
more than what settles into the brain, mind
lost, mind found in the summer palace, walking
along, following a man painting the sidewalk
for tourists, each stroke born in a center
between his ears, rippling out from his fingers,
the knife gone, my eyes pulled back, opened
the way angels tip open the speck of a body
to pour in the soul, and my soul sat up, afraid
to believe it had been let loose in a place so far
from where it began, set loose to walk backward,
follow the lines of thought to where a blossom
lifts its head and thrives where flowers die.

Where We Are Born

Swallow, say the name of the place so softly
our cheeks slip onto a creek's tongue where
we sit and wonder how dumplings are made,
the whisk of a hand tucking them into pockets

like tiny purses with surprises for taste buds,
or the joy of fingers tickling babies, babies
the word for birds born to sit and wait in nests
that sing brightly like matches clicking fires

to live for a very short time, requiring mercy
hanging in the air above them where worms
fall from the mouths of mothers. Mother,
come back from the dead and hold me now

where skies speak the truth of orphans to say
that you gave birth to me, how that sounds
like mounds of money on fire, or a chorus
of brown calves crying in fields of wet grass.

The Earthquakes in Taiwan

The life of the air melts, a film comes,
a sleep covers our eyes, a god dismisses us

the way black women shake the skies
to mark an angry place until the gods

in interiors of every speck of dust shake
clouds so the tiniest thunderstones crack.

I split open this way, a world quaking
from a split deep inside origins of hurt,

my throat full, tongue stuck, choking
on the sick lust of men, memories

full of fractures, bent the wrong way until
my life is undone inside me, forests

swaying, mountaintops struggling
to come back to being straight, as if

straightness is what will save a mountain.
The end has come, and it will come again

to show us it has broad dominion over what
we call God or Nature, a fusion of what lives

inside the nerve that goes from what is pure
joy to a fear of joy, the nerve that is the seat

of the peace that proves itself to be a lie
so that I want nothing, no one, no knowing

except what I know is me, a man who melts,
falls apart to be repaired in broken spaces.

A Chinese Theory of Strings

The cattle moo and make a muck under their hoofs
just over the fence from where I walk in the mornings,
down to my office over a mile away, and I have not seen
the cattle but must believe all sound is evidence of life.

The minor junctions in the crevices of what makes
things real are spaces where I do not breathe, where
I perch on my toes, suspended at the curb as motorcycles
edge by, broken lines, snakes in Taipei's morning traffic.

Here I can suspend myself in a falling apart, the innards
of everything letting themselves become information's bits,
the unbecoming, invisible nothings making me pure light
or a jazz run with license to be mysteries or vapors.

I avoid the one temple at the corner they say is evil,
a too definite place, an assertion of a mind reveling in
the way a mirror leads us to love the face it shows us,
as we are tempted by our eyes to believe what we see.

In Shi Lin Night Market with My Lover

These are ribbons flapping around us, bright ribbons,
every color, some that she has to tell me because I am
blind to color at the worst times, buying socks or guessing
what she is feeling when her face turns from pale yellow
to disappointment, to fear, wound in the streams of fabric
that give darkness light . . .

                           we count the windows that count us . . .

until there is nothing to see, and we sink down into the white
napkins on the backs of the seats, the tiny televisions next
to the driver.
                 I am Chinese in the mirror
                         Chinese is an endless space in time
                                 where Chinese is what I cannot
       Be.

In one window among the thousands I see the faces
of the uncle who betrayed me, the done thing that made
me a child inside a man, stuck in the claws of incest,
in the one window, the way to a scream that jacks open
my mouth but holds sound hostage, the dry tears of silence
like veins cut open where no blood dares flow, this currency
that paid for my tickets, led me in suspension to fly into
the future and live here a day ahead of what happened
to me when I was too young to know treason.
                 I am Chinese in the mirror
                         Chinese is an endless space in time—

I have come here to be what I cannot be.

At Drunken Moon Lake
閉月羞花*

In a white dress at midnight on Drunken Moon Lake,
she tips around the edge of the pavilion where old men
sit after morning Taiji, the sounds now the pluck

of water from fish fighting the touching down
the moon makes when it sleeps, and we come here
to feed the fish so they will not eat the hero's body

the man who loved China more than life,
some full balance in the way winter is still summer
in Taiwan, your hand whole notes but light against

the way my cheeks fill. I ask where you put
the dumplings we saved to honor what friends honor,
lines that guard us against the agony of losing

one another, all these years somehow painted in fire,
a triptych people will erect in rumors, the last power
in the island, the one that survives gas and electric.

The ghost takes her dress in her fingertips to slide
across the water like an immortal, and when I ask what
difference there is between celestials and the unloved,

a bow breaks, the peeping tom eyes of a bug
fall down, its body breaking on the crisp edges of paper
shredded in the glass, not once but forever.

---

* *bi yue xiu hua: hiding the moon, shaming the flowers;*
   referring to incomparable female beauty

City of Eternal Spring

My mind rises up as the silos of interchanges,
streams, passages of myself in floating layers
so nothing can connect, and I dream emptiness
on ships sailing to new places for new names,
this ship my hands cupped in front of me,
a beggar's bowl, a scooped out moon, a mouth
opened to make noiseless screams, to arrange,
to begin, to break through to stop my arrogance,
believing what I touch, see, feel, hear, taste, make
a case for being alive, so I can stop believing what
happens when a caterpillar dreams itself beautiful.

What cannot be is suddenly what I was made
to believe can never be, fibers growing in illegal
spaces between layers of who I am and I wake
from nightmares that come at night or in the day,
memories of being betrayed gathering like iron
threads to make a prison where fibers of a miracle
of light crack open in a seed inside love to let me
dream a body inside this body with structures
that breathe and know one another so I rise
from thought to be, being beyond thought
with energy as breath, a world with eyes
opening inside the light, inside knowing,
inside oneness that appears when the prison
frees me to know I am not it and it is not me.

II. Exile

The Old Man

On my desk near the window facing the cows
I never see is a photo of Grandmaster Wang,
the King of double broadswords (the Old Man)
a hero who died long after the war, the retreat
to Taiwan, the long hard years between those
who lived on the island and soldiers in boats,
with memories of lost families on the Mainland.

I protect the photograph, keeping the sunlight
dimmed to honor my Chinese heritage, adopted
in the Tien Shan mountains, with legends of a boy
who slept in the snow until his knees bled, a monk
looking out finally to see how much the boy loved
the idea of suffering, hanged the thing inside him
until he was tied to it like a rod for being impaled
or a post to be tied to and whipped senseless.

My mother weighs the photo in heaven where
she waits for me to divine my first dream of life,
of the world, of somehow being born, her giving
me back to the doctors to be filed away alive
in a stainless steel cabinet. Not a nightmare, this
is a gift, the *Yijing* tells me, the sign of the dream
the exact time of my real birth, a lake above a lake,
joy of what mixes with sky, as I turn to study
the Old Man so he will show me the way home.

Noodles in Gong Guan with Godfather

for POD

It is time for another bowl, my stomach says,
and my eyes agree in low baritone, whispering
to Godfather, who says we must wait patiently.

She sits at the counter, the cook, the mother,
the owner of things, to see if our bowls are empty,
and they are, empty and wiped clean with air

sifting around our obedience, and she comes
over with more to eat. *This is my favorite place*,
Godfather says, the man who gave me my name

like wind or air, kind and deep face of a man
who rides his bike through the campus, gliding
under palm trees to beat the way summer claims

your skin here this close to the equator,
or to where things are equal. Here my mother
has come to be Chinese with me, still brown

the way she brought me to life, all thick
with the juice of living inside her without air.
It is real or *zhen de* 真的 the true, genuine

way my family assembles in a place foreign
but familiar, my chopsticks working my fingers
so quickly people ask where I learned to eat.

I learned in a city of pain, the bricks baked
red and hard in some secret place in heaven.

Crushing Peanuts in a Hakka Village

In the afternoon the farmers sleep, the sun
too much in love with its own fire to work,
folks hiding in the house with shades drawn,
visitors creeping in the courtyards built to praise
sunrise, begging prayers at sunset, their shoes
all around us, the blue and white tiles colors
the color blind can remember, the way foam
breaks over waves we are told are blue.

Peanuts are everywhere, spread without touching
so they can dry and not connect in the gossip
that weighs peanuts down to the dull way of drying,
instead of this burning that feels like care, feels like
the prick and tickle when the skin is turning dark
on women in Taipei parks on Sunday who forget
their parasols and wince in the shade, their fear
what beauty fears in the sound of crushed peanuts.

Each nut two teardrops connected in the way
a farmer's thumb and finger press the newborn crop,
make them glad to be anchored in the earth until
the day comes to take everyone home to be eaten,
to be crushed in mealy old mouths and mealy mouths
of children, to be made the wish of superstitions
like the hoodoo of Africa, or the wish of markets
here in the low belly of a dragon song in Chinese.

I step on them with feet rude with wonder,
and when one snaps, the hush from windows takes
me to black hands spreading crushed peanuts,
rootworkers casting spells, so I beg forgiveness.

The working of this juju has no medicine I know.

Tea Plantations and Women in Black

in Taipei

It is dusk in the city and here in the mountains,
inside the thick green way of a place where rain
is breath, and summer mist the gas that lets
you dream of being lost, cast away in a paradise

that is not a paradise for those who live here.
I am too familiar to nightmares that pushed me
here to hide from them, but they sit on the edge
of the sun's light pushing down into morning

in the middle of the Atlantic. The tea comes
with a young woman who stares at me, the black
she has heard of, the black she cannot see, and
we light the fire in the table, hear it puff up.

I am full of reasons, strings of hurt I cannot let
loose here where no one knows the sirens on corners
of black homes, hard hands on the grips of guns,
bullets made for Nat Turner and Gabriel Prosser,

or for me, black man daring to live, black man
following the trance of women tipping on loose
stone tablets of sidewalks in thin, black dresses
under parasols to hide them from the truth.

Meeting Old Friends at Drunken Moon Lake

at National Taiwan University

Seniors huddle under the trees to be cool, doing
Taiji, the joints tickling the way bone grinds bone
until the ecstasy comes, the energy melting the pain,
a circle of women with their radios nearby, Broadway
in a Taipei park *"come rain or shine"* Ginger Rogers
in white with Fred Astaire, his eyes closed, arms
out to me as I slide over the grass still wet with rain
to my place, facing the sun to be more chocolate,
to feel the stiffness go away, and I begin, pray into
the Thirteen Postures, grasping the sparrow's tail,
pulling it each time its tiny legs try to bounce away
from me, dipping my hand with my eyes half closed.
It surrenders, and I push against the roof of the hut
made by the tree branches, pull a branch down, then
push it back again so I can swirl, hand over hand,
and stare into the pond, my hand the head of a crane.

There is a tree suddenly, from nowhere, a hand
on my shoulder to say, *you are back again, old friend,*
and it is Peter trying his English, backing away
so I can move into the dance, tuck my head to step up,
take the short stairs to the moon, let my crane
spread its white wings until it sees itself in the mirror,
touches itself, wing to wing to push down and know
the mirror is no lie. It makes the song of the guitar
playing, the long song like five soft taps on the drum,
the soft shoes of Rogers and Astaire on air, no bodies
to hold them back, no wishes for a career where applause
is the silent snap of cricket on its blade of grass,
a monkey teasing it, jumping away, until I see it now,
take its paw and tease it back, its lover in the mountains
behind us, watching, half afraid, half angry at stillness.

The Long Walk Up to Mao Zedong's Retreat

In the museum that was his house, his books
are on the bed where a woman should be, except
he is not here either, we walk up the steep hill
to the courtyard, the gate looks down to Beijing.

I see the places the fires of the foreigners
did not burn, the stone left from buildings that stood
up to the invasion, and I lean against the gate,
my stomach upside down and full of the unfamiliar.

It is a cold chill over the harmony of mountain
and river, and we take tea against the shivers, old
and young poets, my American tongue now naming
the things it knows, cup, tea, cigarette, sky.

Chinese is the long drive here from the city,
standing next to Sun Wenbo, waiting to start his car,
listening to Zang Di speak of what it is to lead
poets along the riverbanks of metaphor, and I am

the one whistle in poplars in a state far away,
Virginia, where a tall young man finds his baby brother
sleeping in the grass, hiding from school, wakes him
so they can dream of families and sons that go searching.

Buying a History of the Language

in a Beijing bookstore

If there are not enough stars in the sky to count
the years it will take to learn these characters,
do not tell me. The shame of it will make me
put my head down, forever counting my toes.

The lines that contain dynasties and emperors
are in these books, and the clerk tells me the lines
even know the way the idea of ink came to China
before the long march to Manhattan art galleries.

It is a bookstore where the simple act of turning
is something I do in the way of Taiji. I go silent,
remember the spine is the steel axis of my mind,
and mind is a thread turning the navel's wheel.

The silkiness of silence wrapping around steel
is the secret wealth of how I have learned
to move in a place where I am the whole world
of difference, black on black in black in silhouette.

The chatter around me is a music I know in part,
the tones going the five directions, the meaning
like a walk through Baltimore's Bohemia, teasing
the idea of language as soul, some kind of genius.

The Fish We Ate

Before he was food he sang to us,
head hung over the edge of the bag,
a waiter smiling to see our vote.

We toasted another round, bottoms up,
as drinkers do, the Beijing skyline sober
behind the fish's last song out of sea.

The white liquor like moonshine
passed around from hand to mouth to
hand and back to mouths pursing

the way we say the word for *fish*.
Lips stick out, pull back, the tongue
plunges down the way fish jerk back

against a hook. In the fire it takes
to make song from liquor, the fish came
back to us limp, a sacrifice to appetite,

split open on vegetables, the last wish
still there somehow, mouth pursed open,
the *you you* sound of what means fish

now cooked. The child in me saw
the head of a Virginia hog that came
once to our house as a hog's oink

and slept into a jellied thing called
souse, Jell-O with vinegar, mama teasin,
A hog head will let you see Jesus.

On Hearing that Michael Jackson Died

Sciatica is three blocks away, left and across
from the stinky tofu stand, the hot cylinder spinning
stink across Gong Guan, where I meet the nuns
at night so we can bow and whisper *Buddha bless us*,
the evening lights making the place one celebration,
women gossiping in the park, the cars so quiet
we look behind us to keep from hitting them, and
when the motorcycles come, lone bugs torn off
from the swarm of locusts, we remember the dance
of no step, the way to keep going or to stand still,
keeping the secret of not moving the mind, putting
my umbrella in the stand at the Buddhist veggie
eatery, learning to understand the price, to count
the coins into the proper bowl, the only black
and round container for a soul this place can hold,
the rain a thing we hope for when the heat is
more than fire, the heat a world come into ours
from a moon next to a distant planet, light years
and wishes over the edge of the mountains down
in the dragon's belly where every child is a genius
who will grow and add to the world in a way
that does not hurt and hobbling back on this
fundamental nerve, back to the eighth floor, my
giant windows looking to the giant windows
of neighbors, I catch my breath, pat the legs
that have made me know a greater humility, how
I have taken them for granted, not even been so kind
as to ask them to show me how to begin on the toes
and slip backward up into the heel over in grace
over the only moon we will ever know.

MRT

In the long perfect tube of the subway
up and down I am almost the tallest person
standing, looking into the ads, seeing what
I can see in the characters, two mountains,
one atop the other telling us to leave,
two fingers walking along like legs to say
person, like me or all the eyes I think are
staring into my skin, this political black,
a stamp over the real ginger orange my chest
is under the clothes, or the breach from dark
to light that happens if you pull my collar
down, the dark spots under the hair on my back
that is a whole project to see, how I have
to turn around in the mirror before a shower
to twist my spine just enough to see why
I should exfoliate more, and I remember the hair
is from my mother's side, and I remember
my mother was ginger orange like my father.

Being is filling the sack of something, knowing
yourself as a space, having mind take over
everything, ignoring the tubes and liquids
that give it something to drive, the mind driving,
stopped only by pain, and the train keeps pain
away from us, as perfect a machine as Chinese
genius can make, no undue slap against the rails
like Boston's T, or the horror of underground
cities in New York. This is the Swiss ticking
of time in a life where I hide in the language,
bury myself in memorizing a writing that is
the opposite of *abc*, an American born color
like blackness, a curtain holding itself over me,
a talking mirror that lets these staring eyes believe

what American hatred would teach them with
its disciples living here, the white minds who
spread the sickness of the place where I was born.

We slide into a new station, and I turn to see
no one is looking at me, no one is wondering
more than what there is for them to wonder, how
to get to work on time, what work to do, where
to buy the children's shoes, what woman
is sleeping with a husband, what mother is ill,
all the things that take the strings of life and make
embroidery, the ties that connect and bind us,
and I am left with my own feelings, nowhere
to attach them, no bulletin board to post a cause
for despair or anger, locked in the flow this way,
blending in as much as the difference of skin,
hair, measures of difference, each one hanging
a melodic phrase in a symphony or jazz set,
or the single pluck of a *pi-pa*, a mandolin born
where the blues are steel bones moving in silk.

Da Mo Meets Ronald McDonald

In the far off lights that speak to saints,
he heard of the tall man in red-yellow rings,
a clown who is not a clown, a man who
is not a man, a beacon calling to saints,
waking the Buddha so that Da Mo took
the roads down from the cave to the streets
full of students and old men, made his way
in his old clothes and sandals, ignoring fingers
held to noses against the smell of gods
who sit in silence without showers or shaving
for centuries, the years gone by, forests
dying and being born, ignoring the way children
point at dark foreigners and saints like slivers
of light that bounce themselves off from heaven.

Quarter pounders and Big Macs, fries,
the whole carnival of what lines the tubes
inside the heart were there when they met,
Ronald for the moment come to life, sitting
up out of the porcelain way of being a statue,
seeing Taipei's afterlife when night is let down
and men go off to see the women without voice,
children asleep or reading gongfu novels
with flashlights, forgetting the characters
of language, Ronald this watchman, paragon
of stillness, Da Mo the light from India
walking into the eye of China's circular way
of winding around itself, the magpie settling
on the backs of fans, women so beautiful
they shame meadows and green mountains.

The Three Black Goats of Mei Nong

At breakfast the monkeys in the trees behind us
cluster over fruit, families of them rustling
the thick leaves over their hair. We can only see
what hides them, watch them move when the leaves
shudder in a snake pattern rising up the mountain,
the noise the threat of monkeys who will stand up
to humans and speak their rights with hands
that can shoot rocks into our guts like balls
of cannons, so we eat without words on the bench
made of old things of wood, the poor woman
picking up thrown away things on the edge of trees
that know what was here long ago and is gone.

It is the way of aborigines, the people standing
with their boats and spears when strangers come
from Mainland, the aborigine way of being unseen
while seeing all the searching eyes of strangers,
until they are beaten back into mountains and
mountain becomes their name, the name of ghosts—
our hearts grow sick of absence one day, we give
love in the way love looks back at loss and cries.
We clean our bowls, put our chopsticks back
where boiling water will make them virgins again,
the three black goats who butt my door
at night now plop down in their own poop,
making the sly smile of chewing cud.

On Visiting Yu Jian

Kunming, Yunnan Province

In the schoolyard children sing the morning to its feet,
the loud snap of feet in the yard, the rattle of the teachers
tending the flock, and I think of Yu Jian's poems
for children, the way he builds sentinels in the characters,
metal sounding the way metal sounds in bells, alarms
for times to sit up and sit down, to run for cover, hiding
from playmates who want to make you it, and the day
creeps up over to light the gateway to the silk road.

In the park the children are older now, men and women
off from days of work, sitting, listening to the erhu,
small bowl in the lap of the player, handle near the heart,
not far from me, this park where we played as children,
me the night song that drifted over the ocean with the sun
to settle here in a wish to find some home that speaks
in the shattered way ancestors become fractals, beat down
to nothing so the truth can breathe without skin.

We have no claims on who we are but are drifters carried
away by invention to be with one another, instant messages,
four billion telephones the size of hands, invisible strings
of the network crossing over and running through every
fiber of every cell as we cut ourselves, craft the flesh
into something that drives us to a place we have forgotten,
noodles with beef, the fire spice of Kunming food,
breakfast on a veranda where white foreigners wince.

The dark ones walk out of the sun into the broad arch,
tasting history, retracing the steps lost in time, steps that came
here from Tanzania when there was no Tanzania, when
color was not the central nervous system of wars, blood

spilling out of the bodies shot into the moon to search
for water so we can live on the planet we have made heavy
with dreams, the dark ones come to peel back the lies,
to lie down in the grass singing what is native to the tongue.

In Shenyang City

with Bei Ta and Mr.Yu

In the wide air of the walkway to the arch,
all the Manchu ghosts sit around us, watching
what was once theirs, tourists now in imperial
spaces, children chasing kites, vendors selling
water when water flows free in the trails
along the tails of dragons flying in heaven.

At the edge of the river we wash our hands,
the water looking brackish, my hands slippery,
and Bei Ta tells me to be careful not to fall here
where I have to find a memory of how to swim,
my mother and my father looking in from the place
where the dead live, touching me on the shoulder,
pushing me back to a safer place on my heels.

My friends ask if my father remarried, a new
bride to shake off the wife who died young,
the way you rearrange furniture or take old suits
to Goodwill. Walking back from the arch,
I remember the way he traced every memory,
followed the string back to some dream of dying
the way one should die, the wealth of a life
left to go on where children are not thieves.

In the arbor we see a bench looking over
to Taiji players in the shade, we sit to count
leaves turning against plastic bottles, the time
it takes a breeze to land on our faces and die,
and it is too much, the silence, the settled air,
we push back, out under the children's kites.

Eating Vegetarian in Taichung with Chien Cheng-chen

in memory of the earthquake of '99

It is a perfect treaty with slaughters,
nothing eaten except what grows in earth,
with flowers smiling on our tables, smooth
stones to tickle our soles as we walk.

I am reminding myself of the way
the vines climb the hills in patterns,
a set of crowns for absent heads, wishes
for absent dreams, the way rain sings.

If there is one thing I want this place
to know, to think of when it cannot see me,
it might be a jewel in a joint in my finger
where cartilage once was, or the deft way

a bird claims a hollow space in the air,
anything but the sounds of children ushered
out when the ground made the sky tremble,
the earthquake stealing lives barely lived.

III. Memories

Oya at He Nan Temple

The Yoruba say Oya leads Sango, an ego
ahead of him in the sky, thunderstorms
easing out of their breath and blood,
their hearts the drum origins of thunder,
the Qi in their eyes the first lightning,
as I wonder if the rain is the hot sweat
of them making love, tied together,

human flesh now flesh of gods, twirling
into and over one another, into oneness,
into emptiness, the water an orgasm
falling on earth, each drop a drum tap
here in the monastery's upper veranda,
the Pacific on the edge of my tongue,

its ocean deepness leagues of language,
Chomsky's broad mess of what we were
before the words, before God was born.
Around me monks speak in Chinese,
a Chinese I understand when I know
who is speaking, and who is making

the rain fall so thick it is now a curtain
on a stage where we dance and connect
the stories of who we are, the fictions
living in the unconscious, waiting there
to emerge whole and new. We are actors
in the mind of what we do not know,

parables of flesh, a ragged comedy.

Archaeology of Time: The Past

In Taiwan a book spoke to me in a bookstore
with words I did not know, a book with a white cover
to hold photographs of families I might have forgotten,
people from this world where words are not made of letters
like tools or nuts and bolts but of tiny pictures, histories.

I paid for the book with lives I do not remember,
handed a fee over to someone bigger than the haunting
that flew me here to where I live in a tomorrow that never
lets yesterday touch what has not happened, a tomorrow
I do not want my black family of my blood to ever know.

The book shows me new families, Chinese people pulled
into sameness of another shared blood, people accepted,
adopted, the way I am adopting this side of time to make
what makes tribes, generations, cities, angry shouts, wars,
love between sheets that hold secrets of who we sleep with.

When the book is open, I have no regrets of family, no wish
to make the past disappear. I am free to choose the possible
here in my own tomorrow, twelve thousand miles from horrors,
from what I used to know to what I can choose to remember,
lives I might have lived with all of my necessary secrets.

It is no secret that one day I will go back to yesterday,
my son meeting me at Logan, the airport with a cowboy name
from a western film where men are violent saints with guns.
With his video camera my son captures the father who left him,
who is now back to make peace with what we call *the past*.

Archaeology of Time: Returning

Auntie Mei left Shanghai to follow
the trail to Gold Mountain, her ticket

bought by a rich man who owned
a laundry in San Francisco where

the sun left America to bring gold
to China, the foreign air of richness,

gold-covered eyeglasses, she turned
her head to say *goodbye* to heartache,

a birthright of Chinese women bound
to the pages of books of wisdom.

We kept a picture of her when she was
a young woman with a mind the gods

made too big for this world, a picture
that was all we had as the days passed

without a word from Gold Mountain,
again a woman deprived of emptiness.

Archaeology of Time: Convertibles

Head thrown back, convertible top
down, radio blasting Louis Armstrong,

driving into Shenyang City, the girls
one smile across the sky, Shenyang

fading into Nashville, *Put a little*
sugar in my bowl, come on, be sweet

in Mandarin, like money on the tongue,
money foreigners bring from whiteness

to trouble the blues veil in Mississippi,
stories we forget on the road at night

with stars that say they will keep pain
away, mark the road with spirits to march

sadness off into the woods and snuff it
out, *O Jesus, why did you leave Buddha*

in the market haggling with women selling
the whole cloth of the end of the world,

cloth we tear to shreds to weave again
into the mesh of black and yellow, a pale

messiah of flat fifths, fingers tapping
pulling our skin over oceans to save it.

Archaeology of Time: Gambling

On a boat bound for Macau, uncle
with his second wife stood confident,

the tables waiting for him, his sure hands,
one on his wife's smile in his heart, one

sliding back across the smooth cloth
to the cards. The war was far away

in places where battle sounds surrendered
to ordinary pleasures, sex and the chance,

the gambler's chance to break through
to where a win is guaranteed, but chance

is a drug, and the sure thing takes away
the thrill of losing everything, falling.

How much of this I remember, how much
I know is about the chance of being born

to a life in a city of shipyards and mills,
sailors, workers with days off from life,

a good uncle who took me to Pimlico,
with the Preakness ground in the smell

of tickets torn up, thrown to the ground,
light flashing and breaking in the panes

of the grandstands, my uncle grounding
me in the wisdom of men the way I sat

on a plane remembering three wives,
bound for Macau, China ripping open,

a heart torn by its own envy in mirrors,
hiding a royal flush, hearts in the blinds.

Archaeology of Time: Stations

Mother cried to think I would love
a woman she could not talk to, a woman

with Cantonese all over the dresses
she said were the best from Hong Kong,

Mother sneering, pulling her tongue back
on the Mandarin way of saying cheap,

cheap cloth, cheap woman for her son,
the kind prince to be lord of the family,

and she took to her bed, feigning death
threatening to join the ancestors, convince

them all to pull their blessings back until
her one good son came to his good senses,

came to understand his station above
where this woman was born, where she

will always be, so constant is the will
of women who bring sons into the world

with a love that commands, that issues
the future across the currants of history,

so the Immortals remind us birth and death
are one thing, unlike love with its stations.

In this life, black me with my black mother
crying to think her prince was casting pearls

across a sea of the unworthy people,
folk who could not do what I could do,

break light or leap across the pages of time
and build disaster into fortune, and back

again with a self-fulfilling mind she gave
me one evening when her water broke.

She saw the place where birth and death
are the wide gate, a shimmering silence.

Archaeology of Time: Shadows

In the change it is dance that gives
glass the sound of music when it breaks,

tinkle tankle becoming crick crack,
soft face in soft face, eye to eye

now the sliver of being opened to light,
surrendering to the fine air of fish as if

fish have no air, and in the change
change becomes a place where the soul

accounts for itself and applies to renew
in a forest in spring or under the weight

of burning cars, perhaps just for a minute,
as if to glance around, remembering even

everything it just lived, like four women
erased in shrieking and crying in Nanjing

go into one man or they stay in soul space
and one becomes my poor mother working

in Baltimore where the mills send a gray
applause to the sky, the music a blues

pasted over with the memories of an erhu
sending songs of ache longing to be ache.

Archaeology of Time: Waste

Everything that was young went quickly,
the way his eyes met mine as soon as we

woke together in a room outside Nanjing,
feeling as if all the things that were falling

would fall and make their thunder, leave
us with the challenge of being happy,

all the things that felt given when gifts
were not just surprises, but what we

knew, what we hoped to take with us
to heaven, unbound by faults and sins,

not deceived the way we were when
the end came to what we knew of China,

landing me here. I am a wish in the skies
spun out from celestial space to be poor,

to be covered with black skin, a felt
quilt of a map with only one way to China—

through pain as big as hogs squealing
at killing time on black farms in Alabama—

the noise of death, the shrill needle
that turns clouds over to rip the air

above the cities where people are young
and all that is given is never taken away.

Recognition

In the rough arithmetic of clipping my toenails
on a piece of newspaper, rubbing alcohol by the bed,
taking no tea for the fever, driving the car after a fresh rain
to watch the shine of the hood in new suns, poking around
in the back of it to rearrange precious things that look like
junk to strangers, as if there is some nosy lens that knows
the precious, or the broad ambiguity of lines that divide us
on maps where the moon goes unseen and languages
lose their signs, fall down and leave us with what we know,
I am you in these habits, hand and face against emptiness.

I am you sitting in chairs, memories coming back
to fill my bones with you, inform the way I get about,
growing old little by little, trying to enlarge the circles
of mother and father and son, the circles my mother made
for me in the pain of bringing me back from breakdowns
so I can see my birth, the decision mother and child make
to come farther into the place we have already entered,
as a mother's womb is the world. It is the world, and
I am you in this broad but narrow moment of surrender.

IV. Intimacies

A First Love Poem

If I can find a cavern as big as silence
where the soft spot under your small toe
holds the song of who we are, I will name

it the way caverns are named, my fingers
pulling back the thin spaces in the notes
of music waiting for us, until we know it,

until we know this place is who we are
when we share the same way of melting,
two kinds of skin from two lives setting

each other aflame, the way confessions
go naked over the curves of our hips,
and drop to the floor near where a bed

waits for us and destinies wait in sleep
for people to dream into the agreement
with what comes into our empty spaces.

Night Walk in Taipei

for Pen-ning

It is a walk that begins with red beans
we cook in the old room above the theater,
leaving there to walk in the crowds, into
the wet fall of night until we reach the straits
and fly on the night song of silver hair,
two webs of electricity, the moon lit
with the way we make lightning, pluck
stars for an aria from *Peony Pavilion*.

When love meets us, it is a voice in dust
above the edge of Cold Cliff, and we lift up
the hot dish made with hero worship.

Wind and air have forgotten magicians
who can fly beyond the range of compass.
We are free in the broad space of dreaming.

The Abacus Speaks to the End of Geometry

for Mindy

If the fact of something happens more than once,
a man stooping down to get a wrench or screwdriver
for fixing something, then fixing a nebulous school
of fish cast out of their home reef to wander to where
water appears in the rain drops of a broken windshield
and this happens just as the man fixing things looks
up and down into the drying water drops from skies
to see the fish again, now microscopic, smaller than fish
are when life is free of menace, and he sees they see
him standing there and believe him to be a woman.

These are the signs of life, the glad testimonies
brought back by the dead when they are born again
to people who have not had the time nor the teachers
to learn stories that became great before the end came
and death was all there was of life, before everything
became new. Now all is new, time again for myths,
for naming the things we do so we forget our actions
until frames of the meaningless claim their meaning.

Cold Mountain and the Maiden

In the way mud oozes through the toes
of children running in the rain, he slides
into Starbucks, the most unkind mark
of history, Mandarin the only gesture
he knows is China, and she comes soon
after, in the glow, leaning against him,
not knowing immortal skin, immortal air.

Time tells him to tell her, and he puts
a spell into things, names this the moment
to tell all, to list the lines in the walls
of the cave, to give out the secret of life,
how it winds itself into us, spins itself
out of us, the prime number key to heaven
and nothingness. In his eyes, she sees
madness, the too still deepness, rude hair,
unkempt way of a Chinese she has never
known, falling into the spell, coffee made
all around her, latte, mocha, caramel,
every caffeine blessing, the patrons
blind to the sage in the homeless man.

He takes her to a table, pulls her down
to the chair with one finger, his breath
cloaking itself in some spring fantasy
hiding the mouth with no teeth, the hands
gnarled from walking sticks with handles
crude the way laughter in the mountains
ignores the rules of manners, the city
now like cities he knows, his spell a law
that brings back the simple ring of things,

night bells in the neighborhood, the toll
of old bones tapping stones in walkways
where the new cries out for what is gone.

Night at the Opera

for Rene

In the Globe the oranges were the oranges
we have here, the clamor the clamor I hear,
men older than me with their walking canes.

In the scroll the characters come to dance
with the singing, one martial actor is a sashay
who sees me, comes closer to taunt and dance.

The general's whip goes into motion, and
all the renegade horses ride again in a dream
of Thulani Davis, her libretto for Malcolm X.

I am lost, my hands as tiny as Fig Newtons
now in a babe's toyland, and I feel the walls
along the place that a question becomes,

as knowing is a place too, these temples
inside us. An aria is an aria but not so here
where the spiraling up and down is history.

We are woven around the core of ritual,
these chairs as hard as pecans after the fall
from trees, grace a wicked smile in the glass.

What the Rains Bring

Wishes granted, sliding back under the sheets,
turning over to kiss one more time, the wall
a wet leaf opening the deep green, a world

that sifts itself into mist. In every slight inch
of the wall of what comes down, I go deeper,
your hand slides down to calm me, circles

of fingers under the fin of fish in the pond,
the figure of rain making tiny stocking caps
that live only for a second in the clarity of water.

In the night women come out in sandals so thin
they have no soles, they hunt for the unattached
eyes of men, collect the favors that make steam

where dust and hot breath have given way
to what must be. I make a valley with my hands
and you touch me one nipple at a time, centers

like the eye that lets rain believe it can blind us
until it hits the earth, and we make it our own,
reason it down until sharp bursts go flying out

to make the veil of water surrender, worn down
with what longing comes to. We pray for rain,
the way it sounds the human to make us real.

A Dream

The last tug at the sleeve lets her blouse fall
off shoulders to breasts that have never seen
a lover, she shudders, shakes so hard I touch

the bones inside the song of this afternoon
to stop the loud way our fear of us rattles her
in the flutter of bugs so fragile they can tear

in the wind. I give her a kiss like a ghost,
a ghost who proves shadows have souls,
bodies that fill with the breath she breathes,

with the ache to touch. Is it a dream of lust,
or the real sex of love, naked and sweating,
a Chinese aria letting its tongue know jazz?

This is the secret—one afternoon in Taipei
she let me, a man of dust, fill her head to toe,
the sound of the city thick with taboos.

America, a Challenge to Love

for Joyce

We undo tiny things, noise of a baby ant picking
at air, in the clump of grass, what the knoll knows,
as if the knoll belongs, its thin places swollen like
gluttons bracing for false gums, what aches when teeth
awaken to the fact of being abandoned, the raw truth
of only tooth to bone like waking up in a nightmare
that replaces grocery shopping, getting a haircut,
losing your sex organ in intercourse, the open air
facts we'd rather not know, the obvious not-being
lying beneath the skin in autopsies on YouTube,
making fun of Dr. Frankenstein to say *it's alive*,
knowing to say so is to lie about what lives if it really
is alive because nothing like that can live, insincere
sense of smiles hiding the next move on the board
where we gather, which has to be small or has
to be nothing, a place where emptiness draws out
desire hidden in a fantasy called friendship, *rock me
until midnight is gone*, while a cup as light as air
holds the unloved, the tiny things swirling inside us.

Nice to Meet You

for Hsing Hui

A thing as delicious as turning the last sound I heard
into a word it cannot be or calling your hidden wish
out into the broad space of the public to make you touch
me instead of asking that I go naked, a thing as delicious
as any of that would not be as safe as a dumb silence.

I am resting my back with a cushion against the chair,
sitting inside the ache when I soaked myself in a balm
the way women went to the river and held things down
until they were as wet as Jesus hanging in the rain,
his pain the invocation of roars destroying the temple.

The things I know are not the things you wish to know,
or they are and I cannot give them to you until I see
what you think of contracts, of what binds the mornings
to unkind sunlight, what takes a hawk and lets it know
there are things less grand than flying, things that crave.

Walking to the Tree of Ancestors

for Pen-ning

The book of one hundred characters guides me,
a children's Rosetta stone, the paces in the street
I count to remember when to turn, across
from the restaurant where everyone goes, the ladies
looking out to call me with their eyes, sirens.

It is a tree where hundreds and thousands
of souls are all souls, everyone in all heavens,
the mind above the great mind of the *Yijing*,
our celestial accounting book where the immortals
note every way a hundred or a thousand can be.

I see the leaves of it now, around the corner,
they are all there is, the voices silent, the chatter
of motorcycles nothing, the drum conundrum
of heat now the still hand on the drum's skin,
the great wish of spirit that made trees go

silent as I sit in prayer with fried dumplings
and a poem full of hundreds and thousands—
sum of what the still wish of loneliness can be.

V. Soul Space

Daoist Festival of the Great Pig

for Robert and Lanshin

Priests in baseball caps carry the gods,
Matzu in her carriage, tiny as Barbie,
as large as the first day of the world.

They light the fires under the stones,
a cool day in a Taiwan winter, the film
of heat tilting us on our heels until we smile.

It is the great pig's day, we missed the pig
but are here to see what Daoists do in secret,
how they open the trapdoor to heaven.

The ladder of knives is just after the fire,
an old priest tapping his feet from hot stone
to hot stone, tap dancing his way to the ladder

where on the rungs of knives he is an acrobat,
while the young priest shakes, clings to the pole,
afraid of the blade slitting the sole, the blood.

The priests in baseball caps smoke, puffing
cigarettes made in America, the caps back
on their heads a little, the sky full of clouds.

Unspoken

I saw my faith
riding on the light
in the ocean one
morning when
the sound of waves
breaking broke me,
I knew the weight
of what is too much
to try to see, each
sparkle in the light
the infinite space
inside the invisible
that lives in me and
will not surrender
itself to naming.

Flux

I am a city of bones
deep inside my marrow,
a song in electric chords,
decrescendo to mute, rise
to white noise, half silences
in a blank harmony as all
comes to nothing, my eyes
the central fire of my soul,
yellow, orange, red—gone
in an instant and then back
when I am, for a glimpse,
as precise as a bird's breath,
when I am perfect, undone
by hope when hope will not
listen, the moon wasting
to where I need not worry
that bones turn to ash,
a brittle staccato in dust.

Mind

In pieces scattered
on the floor of nothing
no determination, no
will could jiggle me
back to being whole until
I surrendered to hurt
to let it rule my actions,
what time to awake,
what time to wash,
what time to cry out
against me hurting me,
sirens of self-abuse,
what time to beg origins
to show themselves
when loneliness was me
feeling my soul the way
a carpenter touches air
as if he can make wood,
it was then my mind
appeared to me, a new
thing that made the making
of things the sacred art
it is, and I learned to live
inside my own sex again.

Kings

Beaten down to bow down
to myself, I had to teach
my own hands to let me go.

Mirrors

We pull ourselves open,
oranges exposed as flesh,
the pungent smell
of being closed too long
something of a surprise.
Have we been ripe without
knowing and forgotten
to take ourselves as serious,
lie down on harsher things
to be opened by wiser hands
than our own? The oranges
we are spell time in ways
our closed selves cannot
imagine, pain goes hollow
and then full again the way
electric storms fill the sky
suddenly and then bring
only light, the rain a tease.

Space

I think myself thin until
a scale calls me to honesty,
its numbers the mind of God,
unrelenting, and I question
a machine that can drive us
to uncertainty, to suicide,
or into the edges of murder,
thinking we are more or less
not there or here. One day
I walked down a street feeling
myself there, feeling as thick
or thin as I wanted to be, light
suddenly a web of shadows made
by utility wires, trees, lines
connecting houses to houses,
as if purpose itself is a thing
we have to assemble, a puzzle
with keys in lives we lived
in other worlds. We have
no weight on those days,
we make no impression
in this world, wherever it is.
I was there as I am here
in what we dream or imagine
ourselves to be, our voices
coming to nothing in a planet
untamed by hallelujahs.

Truth

It was as hot as what
stars must feel like
so far away, certainly
there, inside me.

I took it in my hands,
put it where it should be
in the wet softness
where my heart sits.

Ugly things came
to threaten me, to say
I had lost the last lock
holding me to truth.

That was not true,
because old truths
were now lies, I saw
families as human.

I found the goodness
in what is not perfect,
and a new perfection
in what is not good.

This happened in
a new home twelve
time zones away, as
the world collapsed.

in a clitter clatter
like a busy kitchen,
the universe forming
now inside all of me.

Nerves

My mother says
Boy, go somewhere
and rest your nerves.

My nerves gather
on the bottom of me,
my bottom of my sea.

In Taiji the sea
is where things wait
for the needle.

The needle is
a sharp thing that
can take or give.

The sea's bottom
is where the Qi
rolls out in waves.

These are things
only Daoist Sages
know and feel.

My sage mother
sagaciously says
Boy, go somewhere
and rest your nerves.

Du Fu to Li Bai

I think of how fire rises up
when dead grass is enflamed
the way fear shadows a poet

the bright betrayal of loneliness
creeping in to be with us both,
how it lives inside the poem,

with my family, with your lovers.
I think how we breathe shallow air
at night against the price of fame.

Homesickness

for Yu Kwangchung and Zheng Chouyu

In the mountains a poet can be honest, the city
of poets far below, one head pushing up over another,
while here the only demon is the rain and mudslides,
the tongues of earth water makes with mud that licks
down the edges, pushes over the cars, drowns the voices
of children, the poet's heart busy with what is leaving
the world, what is coming in, time the gift a wife
brings when she cooks and pulls you away from paper

and ink when death creeps nearer and time is all,
time the slip of you into her, your children grown,
gone down into the cities beneath your skin.

We wait these years, count the advantage of the sun
crossing over to Fukien, Matzu, mother of the seas,
watching for swimmers, old soldiers heading home.

The Workers in Beijing

Spring 2005

It is lunchtime, say the feet clomping out from
tarpaulins, metal riggings, walls in progress, men
with blue hats in their hands, clothes thick with work.

In China this hard march to uplift and wealth
is called *the time of cruelty*, mandatory twelve
hour shifts, a mouth of a gift horse for the poor.

They pass me frozen in the intersection,
it is time for lunch and I reach for my brown bag,
fried chicken sandwich, sweet potato pie, a cup

of coffee on the top of the heater in the steel mill,
somewhere in my pocket a hidden book speaks—
Three Negro Classics, DuBois looking ahead

of me to now, my mecca to China, the math
of fifteen years of factory life coming to a dance
between three and five, the three the way things

come to be as the immortals dream of the *Yijing*
way to reality, the oracle of all change, a thin
Howling Wolf looking for peace inside the blues,

where five is the flattened fifth or the five tones
of this language of hand and ache, the rhythm
of my life, my worker heart a lotus pond

in Hainan, the water murky, the sun an unsure
but steady nuclear fume that breathes a sting into
spring, with daffodils, with children who do not die.

Some whistle blows, I go back down under
with these men I do not know, singing a song
my father sang—*fifteen years ain't no long time*

I got a brother somewhere got a lifetime.

Being Chinese

In Los Angeles airport I sit
stunned by the English, letters
harsh things with no stories
I know. The food smells dead,
metal forks and knives set
for making war against food.

I am undone and done again,
broken off from narratives
of birth and being, of limits
broken by the genius of slaves.
I stand here where I was born,
and the masks wait for me.

Notes

City of Eternal Spring concludes the trilogy that began with *The Plum Flower Dance. The Government of Nature* was the second book in the trilogy. The title poem "City of Eternal Spring" is inspired by chapter 26 of the *Dao De Jing*, a portion of which announces the theme of *The Government of Nature.*

As it appears on the cover, the author's Chinese name, Wei Yafeng 蔚雅風, was given to him by Dr. Chinghsi Perng, professor emeritus of National Taiwan University, during his tenure as a Fulbright Scholar in Taiwan.

The Chinese poem in the front matter is an original poem by the author. It is likewise inspired by chapter 26 of the *Dao De Jing*. The poem may be paraphrased as follows: So that I might hear the quiet voice of the union of heart and mind, help me forget the past and the future.

In 2002 the author received an appointment from the Fulbright Association to teach at National Taiwan University and Taipei National University of the Arts in Taipei, Taiwan, for the spring semester. He also began his daily practice of Daoist sitting meditation at that time. Inspired by an initiative from the Fulbright offices, the author began studying Mandarin toward the project of deepening his understanding of Chinese culture and working with poets in China, Taiwan, and Hong Kong. He subsequently convened two international conferences (2004, 2008) on Chinese poetry at Simmons College. His guests included prominent Chinese poets from China, Taiwan, Hong Kong, and the United States.

A significant section of this manuscript was completed while the author was a resident at the Renaissance House Writers' Retreat in Oak Bluffs on Martha's Vineyard. "The Old Man" is about the late Wang Chueh Jen (1910–1990), a martial artist and veteran of the Chinese Civil War who was known as one of the Five Tigers of Taiwan, martial artists whose skill was uniformly regarded as superior. He was the sixty-third grandmaster of the Tien Shan P'ai system. The author is one of a few Dao disciples in the Tien Shan P'ai system.

The poem "Da Mo Meets Ronald McDonald" is about Da Mo, 達摩, a monk from India who is said to have been the first patriarch of Chinese Buddhism. The influence of Daoism on Buddhism is said to have produced Chan or Zen, as it is commonly called in the West.

The poems in part III, "Memories," were inspired by a collection of photographs taken from an archive of twentieth-century Chinese apparel entitled *Old Photographs* published by Jiangsu Fine Arts Publishing House.

In the poem "Night Walk in Taipei," *Peony Pavilion* (*Mudan Ting*) is the famous Ming Dynasty romantic play that is part of the repertoire of most Kunqu traditional opera troupes.

In the poem "Flux," the phrase "city of bones" is a reference to *Gem of the Ocean*, a play by August Wilson.

In "Being Chinese" the reference is to a period of eight months in the author's sabbatical year (2004–2005) when he lived in Taiwan and studied Mandarin at the Taipei Language Institute. He returned to North America briefly to attend AWP in Vancouver but was otherwise living in Taiwan. He also traveled in mainland China during that time.

In 1973 the author received his first copy of the *Dao De Jing* by Gia-fu Feng with photographs by Jane English, and in 1978 he began his studies of Taijiquan and internal development in Tien Shan P'ai while living in his native Baltimore, where from 1970 to 1985 he worked in factories. He holds a first-degree black sash in Taijiquan from the World Kuoshu Federation and is one of several disciples in the Tien Shan P'ai Association under Huang Chien Liang, the sixty-fourth generation grandmaster.

Acknowledgments

The author would like to thank the editors of the following journals for publishing these poems, sometimes in earlier versions or with other titles:

Academy of American Poets: "Flux"; *Asian American Literary Review*: "What the Lotus Said," "The Three Black Goats of Mei Nong," "Crushing Peanuts in a Hakka Village," "On Hearing that Michael Jackson Died," "MRT," "On Walking to the Hundred Year Old Tree," "At Drunken Moon Lake," and "The Workers in Beijing"; *Cossack Review*: "Buying a History of the Language" and "The Fish We Ate"; *Ploughshares*: "A Dream" and "Space"; *Poet Lore*: "Recognition"; *Poetry*: "Waste"; *Rumpus*: "City of Eternal Spring"; *Terminus*: "America, a Challenge to Love" and "Cold Mountain and the Maiden"; *Transition Magazine*: "Eating Vegetarian in Taichung with Chien Cheng-chen"; *Tupelo Quarterly*: "The Abacus Speaks to the End of the Century," "Unspoken," and "Mirrors."